I want to be a SALES CLERK

By Eugene Baker

Illustrations by Carol Rogers

 CHILDRENS PRESS, CHICAGO

Library of Congress Catalog Card Number: 74-79579

Copyright ©, 1969, Regensteiner Publishing Enterprises, Inc.
All rights reserved. Printed in the U.S.A.
Published simultaneously in Canada

3 4 5 6 7 8 9 10 11 12 13 14 15 16 17 18 19 20 21 22 23 24 25 R 75 74 73 72 71

The children in
Miss Lee's room liked
books about pioneers.
That is how it
started.

On Monday, Tim made
a log cabin on a table.

On Tuesday, Sam and
Andy made trees. They
used paper and sponges.
"Now this cabin is
in a forest," said Sam.
Andy put some little
animals in the forest.

On Wednesday, Jill
made a man and a woman
out of clothespins.
"They live in the
cabin and hunt for food
in the forest," she said.

On Thursday, Mary made a lake with a piece of mirror.

"Now the man and woman can have fish, too," she said.

It was fun to build this pioneer home. The children loved doing it.

But on Friday, Joe cut down some of the trees.

"Oh, how could you?" cried Sue. Everybody was angry with Joe.

"Pioneers did not eat just fish and animals," said Joe. "They made vegetable gardens. They cut down trees so they could plant a field of corn."

"Pioneers had no stores," said Miss Lee. "They wove cloth for their clothes. They made their shoes and soap and candles. They also ground their grain to make flour."

"But," said Jane, "how did stores begin?"

"Let's find out," said Miss Lee.

Tim found out
about trading posts.
  A trading post was
a kind of store. Indians
traded furs for knives,
traps, cloth, and guns.
  Sometimes pioneers
came a long way to trade
things they had for other
things they needed.

Sam found out
about the peddler and
his wagon.

The peddler had
many things that the
people needed. He
had big iron kettles
and spinning wheels.
He had tools and iron
candle molds. He
brought his wagon-store
to the people.

Andy found out
something else.

"When more pioneers
came," he said, "a town
grew. The peddler did
not have to travel. He
settled down and opened
a store."

Jill said, "When the towns grew big, there were all kinds of stores. Some sold food. Some

sold shoes. Some sold
hats. Some great big
stores sold everything.
They still do!"

"Big stores don't sell EVERYTHING," said Mary.

"Why don't you girls visit a big store and find out?" said Miss Lee.

"My sister, Ann, is a sales clerk in a big store," said Mary. "We will go to see her."

They went on Saturday.

The big store was a bright and busy place.

They found Mary's
sister in the place
where lamps were sold.

"Do you have any
candle molds?" asked
Mary.

"Candle molds! No
we don't have any candle
molds," said Ann.

"See," said Mary.
"Big stores do not have
everything."

"We try to have everything that people want to buy," said Ann. "This is an important part of what a big store tries to do."

"Do you like being a sales clerk?" asked Jill.

"Yes I do. I like people, and I like the things I sell."

"I help women get the right lamps for their homes," said Ann. "I have to know what each lamp costs, and how to write a sales slip. Sometimes I move the lamps around to show them off in a better way. I have to keep well so I won't get too tired, and so I can come to work every day."

"Could I be a sales clerk someday?" asked Jill.

"Yes," said Ann. "There are almost as many jobs as there are kinds of things to sell. You should finish high school. Study your math. You have to add and make change. Some high schools have special classes for people who want to work in stores."

"In a small store,"
said Ann, "the owner would
tell you what to do. Some
big stores have special
training programs."

One day Jill found
a candle mold in her
grandmother's attic. She
put some ivy in it.

"That," she said, "is
to remind me that I will
be a sales clerk in a
store that has the kinds
of things that people want."